MORTAL GEOGRAPHY

The Lexi Rudnitsky First Book Prize in Poetry

The Lexi Rudnitsky First Book Prize in Poetry (formerly the Lexi Rudnistky Poetry Prize) is a collaboration between Persea Books and The Lexi Rudnitsky Poetry Project. It sponsors the annual publication of a poetry collection by an American woman who has yet to publish a full-length book of poems.

Lexi Rudnitsky (1972-2005) grew up outside of Boston. She studied at Brown University and Columbia University, where she wrote poetry and cultivated a profound relationship with a lineage of women poets that extends from Muriel Rukeyser to Heather McHugh. Her own poems exhibit both a playful love of language and a fierce conscience. Her writing appeared in *The Antioch Review, Columbia: A Journal of Literature and Art, The Nation, The New Yorker, The Paris Review, Pequod,* and *The Western Humanities Review*. In 2004, she won the Milton Kessler Memorial Prize for Poetry from Harpur Palate. She is the author of a book of poems, *A Doorless Knocking into Night* (Mid-List Press, 2005).

Lexi died suddenly in 2005, just months after the birth of her first child and the acceptance for publication of her first book of poems, *A Doorless Knocking into Night* (Mid-Lest Press, 2006). The Lexi Rudnitsky Poetry Prize was founded to memorialize her and to promote the type of poet and poetry in which she so spiritedly believed.

Previous winners of the Lexi Rudnitsky First Book Prize in Poetry:

2008 Tara Bray, *Mistaken for Song*
2007 Anne Shaw, *Undertow*
2006 Alena Hairston, *The Logan Topographies*

MORTAL GEOGRAPHY

ALEXANDRA TEAGUE

WINNER OF THE 2009
LEXI RUDNITSKY FIRST
BOOK PRIZE IN POETRY

 A KAREN & MICHAEL BRAZILLER BOOK
PERSEA BOOKS / NEW YORK

Persea Books, Inc.
853 Broadway
New York, NY 10003

Library of Congress Cataloging-in-Publication Data:

Teague, Alexandra, 1974-
Mortal geography : poems / Alexandra Teague. -- 1st ed.
    p. cm.
ISBN 978-0-89255-358-7 (original trade pbk. : alk. paper)
I. Title.
PS3620.E42M67 2010
811'.6--dc22
                                        2009051231

Printed in the U.S.A.
Designed by Lytton Smith
First edition

in loving memory of my mother, Sylvia

Contents

III. Present Perfect

I. Dead Reckoning

Adjectives of Order

That summer, she had a student who was obsessed
with the order of adjectives. A soldier in the South
Vietnamese army, he had been taken prisoner when

Saigon fell. He wanted to know why the order
could not be altered. The sweltering city streets shook
with rockets and helicopters. The city sweltering

streets. On the dusty brown field of the chalkboard,
she wrote: *The mother took warm homemade bread
from the oven. City* is essential to *streets* as *homemade*

is essential to *bread*. He copied this down, but
he wanted to know if his brothers were *lost* before
older, if he worked security at a twenty-story modern

downtown bank or downtown twenty-story modern.
When he first arrived, he did not know enough English
to order a sandwich. He asked her to explain each part

of *Lovely big rectangular old red English Catholic
leather Bible*. Evaluation before size. Age before color.
Nationality before religion. Time before length. Adding

and, one could determine if two adjectives were equal.
After Saigon fell, he had survived nine long years
of torture. Nine *and* long. He knew no other way to say this.

Referral

I had insurance. I had the risk of fair skin.
It was Halloween; a bumblebee checked me in.
She gave me a chart for my family history of cancer.
Leukemia. Yes. Who? My mother. Died at 66.

It was Halloween; a bumblebee checked me in.
Brain cancer. My aunt. I can't remember—young.
Leukemia. Yes. My mother, who died at 66.
I was called into the room before I was ready.

Brain cancer. My father's side. I think she was 37.
I was handed a paper gown; it opened in the back.
The intern called into the room before I was ready.
No history of melanoma. My whole life.

I was a paper doll; my gown opened in the back.
The intern entered; she was dressed up as an intern.
No history of melanoma. My whole life,
but maybe it's getting darker. I was referred.

The intern nodded; she was dressed up as an intern.
She pressed the edges with her purple gloves.
You think it's getting darker? Maybe. I was referred.
(I'd always thought of it as my private continent.)

She pressed the edges with her purple gloves.
Benign, I think, but the doctor may say remove it.
I'd always thought of it as my private continent,
uneven shores eroded by waves before my birth.

Benign. At least for now, no need to remove it,
the doctor said. He stopped a minute at my back's
uneven shores eroded by waves before my birth.
$400. Trick or treat. A pirate took my co-pay.

I had insurance. I had the luck of this fair skin.

Dead Reckoning

in memory of Floyd Berry, my grandfather

His letters arrived each day, even after he died.
Dearest, I love you. We are so lucky to have

had each other for so long, Dearest.
From the fluke of an anchor, August 13, 1944:

I am sitting with my back against the center.
It sounds uncomfortable, I know, Dear,

but it's just like a big chair. For the service,
the chaplain had brought an organ folded

in a large suitcase, *the cutest thing you*
ever saw. Perhaps when I have liberty again,

I'll get to town and get some music. I tried
to play Malagueña last night, and I can't

even start it. It's a shame, but it can't be helped.
He was allowed to write the names of songs

but not of places, and when he crossed out
of their hemisphere—*Yesterday, some of us*

had to wear diapers. Quite a sight, but better
you didn't see, Dear—her sister had to explain.

He'd been reborn a sailor at the world's
center, the equator narrow as a single bunk—

It still seems wrong and strange to sleep
without you, Sweetheart—as smoke

inking the sky above the South Pacific
as the ship exploded. *Darling, even if*

I have to be away for the longest time,
I am coming home to you, just as fast as I can.

The Whole Story of Winter

I believe no natural cold as yet known can arrest travel.
The whole story of winter illustrates it.
—Dr. Kane, Grinnell Expedition, Baffin Bay, 1854

The season was unusually forward that year.
When we awoke, we had lost our reckoning:
seven men, an old copper kettle,
and half-a-dozen bottles of lime juice on a crystal raft.

We did not talk of the men on the *Advance*,
or the purple andromeda we'd burned last spring
below the mer de glace—a river system imperceptibly flowing.
Around our floe, the young ice slewed and tongued,

and Godfrey broke out in "I'm off to Charleston
a little while to stay!" We saw white hummocks resolve
into walls and hedges, frost smoke rising above pastures,
a pinnacled berg convert to a church with spire and belfry.

Within an hour, no open water showed itself for yards.
Wherever placed, our compass needle stood.
Land ice filling the leads,
we pointed the needle south and prayed

our absence was enough to save the rest from scurvy.
The Esquimaux seal hunters walked the sky for days.
Amalatok had told us that in their tongue
all numbers—whether much or little—have one name.

For weeks the stars told us the time of day.
It was nearly noon.

Cave Tours

The underworld the bright brochures have shown
declines our courtesy. The rare albino fish
wait in the falls, and the blind salamanders,
ignoring camera flashes, sulk in cracks.

Even the bats, aloof as specks of mold
on Adam's half-cleaned torso, wake no fears.
High ground, we know, is less than promised—flawed
as a poorly buttressed church whose steeple

we've inhabited for years without angelic
sightings. Perhaps the other angels moved
down here as well. It's best, at least, to know
the holes our faith must skirt or be led into.

Our Virgil says this single room could hold
the Pentagon, pointing his flashlight beam
at *iron curtains*, hemmed with pleated stone.
We've seen all this before with other names,

these forms we grace with shadows. Each time
the lights click on, the novices blush
as though they truly wished their petty sins
kept private; as though our sin were not

that desperation for the timer's lights
to ring the limits of our nothingness.
Centuries old, these stones are still alive.
Someday, the guide explains, these two will meet.

We long to touch them—glistening, infantile,
like space in us too deep inside to heal—
but know our Midas touch is mortal here.
The tarnish on our palms adds up to death.

The Sociologist Dreams

for Karyn

The people she dreams are drowning
all have names created, newly, as theories. Their bodies float in the water.
She reaches to save them, but their hands turn to pages of numbers:

35% of unmarried mothers sink below the line
of poverty; 90% sink below the sea. They are the same
when she writes them.

The boat she cannot right capsizes repeatedly,
the paramedic waiting above a cold staircase of waves. She moves
to a house where the air conditioner leaks

and the girls next door wear negligees in the street: .2% of women
turn tricks at some point in their lives, or is it 2% or only 2
in their raveling pink slips, who look her boyfriend first down

then up? He tells her people must become anonymous
to recognize themselves; he reads aloud an article on a child who sees math
as color: 7s green, 9s blue. This proves the substance of numbers,

their divisibility into fractions of light.
No, she says, *wrong numbers aren't clear as misspellings:*
out of context, 372 looks as right as 273 or 32.

Sometimes, the boat balances on its masts, then turns upright
and sinks. She suspects they are using bodies as ballast. She says so twice
because here she says everything twice

and the paramedic answers once-too-few times: *It'll be all right.*
She realizes he is reading a manual.

25% of the homeless are insane, and one of the signs
is believing the same words mean something different each time.
What about believing the same words mean something the same?

Isn't this, the paramedic asks, what you wanted? To save people?
They'll leave off their names on the form; they'll fill in their ages:
the 76% who are literate, not counting the 94% who can't
  write on waves.

What would you say this means? he asks her.
She finds herself saying, *Nothing at all.* She finds herself saying
nothing at all.

Notes from the Twelfth Week

The portion of some is to have their afflictions by drops,
now one drop and then another; but the dregs of the cup,
the wine of astonishment, like a sweeping rain that leaveth
no food, did the Lord prepare to be my portion.
—Mary Rowlandson, Captivity Narrative, May 1676

You ask me to describe the child. It is dead.
You who did not watch the sagamore dance with shillings at his knees,
you who did not kneel nine days with death in your lap.
You, who they said would die.

But, my good husband, the bay was not burning.

What can I tell you of the snow? Her fever burned it from my hands.
She was all night growing cold. I would have carried her body.
They buried it upon a hill some hours while I was sent for.

My master's hands were darker than the earth on fire,
darker than our house falling in on itself.
My sister cried, *And Lord, let me die with them,* and died.
I will tell you, they gave me a Bible as comfort. *Come, behold*

the works of the Lord. I read God's curses on that brow,
the shadows circling the skin. Our Mary had been sold for a gun.
Who could I have said would save us?

You who do not watch the man crawl the red earth of this bed chamber,
whose hands lie folded on this stranger's quilt each night.

Already, you praise me for kneeling in snow
you did not see stained. You ask me which prayers I favored.
I gathered groundnuts in broken baskets.

I have sent thanks to Mrs. Usher and the gentleman of Boston
for the twenty pounds. I am alive, lying always

between your eyes and God's. It could not be otherwise.
The neighbors wonder at my election: their whispers are drops of rain.

There have been signs, surely.

Caesarean

*It is a better omen when the mother dies in giving birth
to the child; the first of the Caesars. . . got that name
from the surgical operation performed on his mother.*
—Pliny the Elder

To be born from a corpse, cut darkly toward breath,
like spirit unsewn from the cloth of death,
was fortunate. The midwives held open his mother's lips
to give the child air. Below the knife that slipped
across his crown, the *caesus* parted like a mouth
that babbled senseless blood into the shock
of pale cloths. Who knew what woman's flesh might say?
The boy lay safe. Still, someone would lace
her closed—the waspish needles stinging down the wound.
Now, midwives un-cord the son whose sons
will found green empires over knotted roots,
the old vines yielding new, more potent fruit.

The Eucharist

after a photograph by W. Eugene Smith

*Beneath the most familiar of appearances—a crust
of bread—a god is devoured.* —Jean Genet

Genet would have liked this scene—its ritual profaned
by a camera; the hushed black and white church
somewhere in the Philippines, where incense stings
tears to the porcelain eyes of the saints;

two plaster angels praying in the wings
for flight, a gust of wind to lift
the priest's black robe, the cross on his back
flapping up in confused ascension.

One altar boy glances back, an impish swap:
immortality for a negative.

Only he and the burned soldier stare out,
the man they carried in before the shot to wrap
in cotton. Bound now, he cannot move, only blink
when the flash goes off, the white light
like some distant fire or heaven.

Beside him, a veiled woman perches on a cot,
her head bowed down, eyes fixed on the bare feet
of the woman kneeling before her. Their brown soles
are split as if she's walked for days to look away,

as all the pious do, while bombs clink
prisms on the chandelier, the camera clicks, and God's bones crack
inside the priest's soft mouth.

Hiking Through: The John Muir Trail

It is true, we are but faint-hearted crusaders, even the walkers,
nowadays, who undertake no persevering, never-ending enterprises.
—Henry David Thoreau

It's true 220 miles will end after 220
miles of walking, figuring the ratio
of miles to rations of food, refiguring
pounds of food still carried, food not
carried, its pounds too many for miles
to be walked, reconfiguring the miles
into hours of light divided by hours
already walking; hunger prefiguring
the hours spent dreaming of food.

> *You are deep-frying everything in your friend's kitchen:*
> *two loaves of bread, salmon, apples, corn on the cob,*
> *potatoes, steak, sticks of butter glistening and sizzling in oil.*

The lakes hold clutches of small islands,
shores inside shores, insects in blue amber.
The lakes are women. Marjorie. Marie. Ruby.
Virginia. *Thank you for your wine, California;*
thank you for your sweet and bitter fruits. Muir,
Mather, Glen. The men are talus peaks
and passes. A new vocabulary: before you
summit, you must *stage*. This scene begins
by a lake; you soak blisters big as your toes.

> *Apple pie; peach pie; rhubarb pie; cherry pie; apricot pie;*
> *blueberry pie.*

One line read in fifteen days—*For in what
does time differ from eternity except we measure it*—
measure of comfort on a granite shelf.
Time that can be divided can be added:
scrabble of rockslide to descent. One
red line through thirteen topos. Forests
burned to flagpoles. *After what seems like
an eternity, the grade eases*, the guidebook's
promise. Waterproof lakes become water.

> *You are at a buffet. All-you-can-eat saag paneer, aloo paneer,
> matar paneer, naan, pakoras, samosas, raita, and halva.
> You spend the whole night looking for a plate.*

Whitney resurveyed the range and moved
his name to the highest spire. Imagine
belonging to altitude alone—the blue balloons
12,000 feet up Mather Pass, a string of trash
from a car lot, bobbing like celestial buoys.
Imagine names given by the trail, by hungers:
Bat-Wing, Five-Leaf Clover, Cucumber Girl,
creatures teeming and swarming as Roosevelt
knew we must into the rich and idle wilds.

> *Dehydrated macaroni and cheese. Energy bar.*

It is hopeless not to think of walking, but
you can think of walking slowly, a rover
a la Sainte Terre, a story told to make all
idle walks seem pious—turned to *sauntering*,
meandering, a burdenless beast out ambling
through the wilds, rambling, promenading,
wandering 220 miles through and to the holy land.
You'll know you have arrived without a map;
the last junction will be stillness with stillness.

Seeing Edward Hopper's *Hotel Room*

after Larry Levis

For years now, she has been sitting on this bed
inside my mind, her knees together
and her chin turned down as though her body were a window
with the shutters closed, and though the room is big enough
for me to step into, and the green chair almost
empty with its padded back, no one will ever sit there.

What I've been waiting to say to her is not even
to her, but to a man who understood
that loss was not a blank wall or a single bed,
but tousles of wheat fields going on
for miles outside an open window.

He knew it's where we're free to go we can't escape.

A horse's leg bones or the old man's mismatched
socks relentlessly lead back to rooms where wasps
swarm in the California dusk like ghosts
of those still living. And if I try to come upon her
like a stranger and see the blinds
three-quarters closed and dull gold as an envelope
or the two suitcases with their upturned, nameless
tag, or try to argue that the check he said she holds
is far too big to be a check, and is instead a letter
folded on itself, a message sent ahead to this hotel
by someone who knew where she would stay
before she did, I cannot make her loss less permanent
or less unreal. Surely she wonders, as we all do,
if her life were not addressed to someone else instead.

Perhaps she holds a poem written by a man
she thought would come and find her here inside this room
inside this palace in Madrid, and though he said
that no one understood her waiting and though the story
he told was someone else's life, she likes the words,
spilled like the rented light across her hands, the paper
draped over her knee, almost a bandage. Now
all she has left of him is all she ever had.

Frames

The fire hoses ruined everything that didn't burn.
Flakes of ash, a forest in our living room, a flood.

We drove all night the day we heard, recalling
what we'd lost before we found it gone.

All my dolls. The plum tree and the blue cathedral.
The Indian scout, painted to a ledge of rock

above the canyon and the couch. For years,
my mother wanted out. She nailed frames

for painters, laid away landscapes and distant
lands, paying check by check. She made a house,

a home. Our history inside a box of photographs.
We were not there to see the flames signaling

dawn behind the fire trucks, neighbors on porches,
half asleep. We climbed in through a broken window,

crossed the wet black moss that had been carpet.
Moss of ash, a distant landscape in our living room, a ledge.

We drove in ruins after we heard. We were not home
to see the fire trucks through a burning window,

plum fire signaling above the canyon and the rock.
The Indian scout half slept inside a painter's history.

For years, my mother wanted a cathedral.
She climbed into a house—a box, nailed

check by check. She laid blue carpet, painted, paid
for couches, broken dolls. She founded a land

of photographs. We lost it all. Hoses flooding
the porch; neighbors behind the trees—a forest

of flame. The day gone wet and black as night,
we crossed the frame, recalling everything.

Genome

Composed of chemical symbols designated by a four-letter alphabet of A's, T's, C's, and G's, the human genome, if printed in standard type, would cover 75,490 pages of this newspaper.
—*The New York Times*, February 2001

Those weeks, we forgot to buy papers, reading
German names on Texas road signs—*Schulenburg: Halfway*

to Everywhere. Live oak, lantana, and one noon,
hexagons of earth lifting up from itself, accidentals

of clover. Below our moving van's fiberglass roof, the bed slats
and cardboard boxes bore the bright, archived glow

of museum pieces. We slept among them at a truck stop
in Arizona where a man with a dog asked for a ride west

in the grey dawn. He had met the Rainbow People in the desert.
We were carrying only what we could not dispossess and said

we were sorry. None of this was new: the motor's churning
like Kerouac's typewriter-paper falls, the truck's imponderable

body, the hours we didn't count until the pink sky
darkened. At the KOA's playground, no one told us

we were closer to fruit flies and mustard plants than ever.
The human genome had unraveled into 30,000, and soon,

the first rhesus monkey would be born with a jellyfish gene.
He would not glow green as expected. We read all this later.

That night, we swung in the cradle of swings.
We listened to the desert's near infinity of noises.

What I Know For Sure

When I look at my abdomen, I see a scar turning
back to lighter skin from where a surgeon cut

five inches across, and just before this, I remember
trying to stop screaming as my intestine ruptured

by reciting names—first middle and last—
of everyone I could think of, though I do not know

for sure if I got all the middle names right,
or if I have ever known yours.

In last Thursday's *Kansas City Star*, I saw a photo
of an x-ray of a man's head imbedded with a nailgun nail

that, according to the story, had missed his eyes
and seven centers of planning and purpose inside

his frontal lobe and done, really, no damage.
The doctors called this a *true miracle*,

which made me think that death does not happen
by cause and effect, though I do not know for sure

that the story or picture or both had not been doctored
to improve circulation, as though printed words

and paper are, the same as us, a living body.
My parents gave me the middle name Rachael

for its numerological value, and my whole name
therefore adds up to seven, which is said to be lucky.

The pre-surgical report describes me as being
of steady age which makes me wonder if some

people's ages are in visible flux.
I do not regularly sign my middle name or initial.

The surgeon recorded cutting me with a *ten blade*
just below McBurney's point.

Even having been opened there,
I do not recognize this name as my body.

Cork

The bus leaves before I can expect it to,
rocking like a child's top on the pitted road

down past the green railings and the grey river,
buildings segmented by color. To our left,

barber shops and a hardware, what might be
the limits of this city which as a child I pictured

as a place that floated, a cylinder of land loosed
from a bottle of wine—ancestors barely,

gloriously balanced. And though I now know
corach meant great marsh, the land seems no

more firm, the cathedral drifting at the city's top
like duckweed. It was built during famine, yet

only the gargoyles are lean. With goat shags
of beards, they must have been carved as demons

pastured in sky, though I think first of my mother's
childhood friend who lived in a tent with a goat,

its milk heavy with the smells of hair and dirt.
My mother learned not to breathe as she drank;

learned how little must keep the body alive
when it's asked. Once, she tricked me with the riddle:

"Which weighs more, a pound of feathers or a pound
of stone?" and for weeks I disbelieved the answer.

Now I think of angels on the head of a pin, souls floating,
souls sinking: the deceptive weight of their feathers.

The Idea of North

after Glenn Gould

These walks on frozen lakes are only practice,
a space for solitude like the hours
you spent with your wrists in steaming water
coaxing music from the raised blue veins.

I circle on the edge and listen to ice crack
loose, a sound like keys struck one by one
by one—tentative notes bled into a darkened
concert hall. Here, as there, the audience

lies mute. Sagegrass, poke, Queen Anne's lace,
rows of white-gold bodies stilled. In the center,
black water rises through, an undercurrent,
like the tune you always hummed, not quite

submerged, below your playing. Was it a sound
you heard on long night walks alone? Snow
suspended like music. Or the memory of Arctic
cold, pages of a score flipped back, a rustle

like geese lifting into the frozen northern sky.
You never played that great concerto.
Maybe those nights you dreamed of touching
someone simple who would listen

as the maid did once in a hotel room in Boston,
the record spinning on a player by the window
while she looked up slowly, something bright
as water rising up through ice inside her eyes.

Explanation to a Student

Even in Shakespeare, some words mean
what they seem; here water is its ordinary self, dripping
no irony, sloshing waves up the shore,
and when Roderigo wants to drown himself

from sorrow, he means, quite literally, drown.
If you do not see a circle floating above the line,
a buoy marking deeper meanings,
notes submerged by ripples of *thous* and *'zounds,*

you may lie on the raft of the surface—
as Roderigo might have, unrequited but still too light
for drowning, or as you would be carried
from your chair if a friend said, *I'd love*

some water. You'd fill her glass with liquid,
tasteless and transparent, not wondering
if she wanted something metaphoric (the boiling point,
viscosity, and surface tension unusually high

for its molecular weight), like tragedy, or love.
When the time comes to navigate
the shoals inside soliloquies, you'll have to trust
not all words will deceive you. Not all are *false*

as water, which you'll remember
Othello calls the dead Desdemona, to explain
why he has killed her, why he would not listen
to her vow she had always been true.

House Guest

Nor is the prophet Elijah the only one to put on the garb of a beggar.
The Angel of Death delights in frightening men in the same way.
—Elie Wiesel, *Dawn*

When he comes to your door, you cannot risk refusal.
You offer warm, crusted breads, hollow and lightly sanded
as coffins; alphabet soup with solar flares of carrots,
penumbras of barley. You were not, you explain,

prepared for a guest. When he lifts the bowl to drink broth,
you try to believe he is not reading and then swallowing
your name. What else can you give as hospitable distraction?
Coffee in a bone china cup? You remind yourself he's come

as a beggar, not a chic reviewer, though by Sunday, you offer
trowel wedges of cucumber sandwich, set his glass on thin
cork. You begin to remember deaths, brief and out-of-context

as postcards: a burro you once saw fight itself dead, trapped
half out of its mother; a neighbor's cat that ate its own kittens;
your grandmother, drugged in a pink bathrobe. You suspect
that you are the beggar—your tin cup of graciousness

empty. And though you say nothing, you find him next morning
making waffles from scratch. He fills their square pillows
with syrup and brews you Earl Grey. In the bathroom, he's left
new soaps wrapped in tissue paper like a nice hotel, washcloths

folded like flowers. You pretend such luxury is natural—each day
more fearfully accustomed to the wings brushing your arm;
you read the paper silently together: first comics, then obits, then news.

No Dominion

In the beginning was the word, and sometimes only the word
was still there at the end, too.
                    —Constantine FitzGibbon, *The Life of Dylan Thomas*

All August, you acrosticked yourself to rhyme backwards
from now to now. Black rot leafed the scarlet forests
of the walls, and Wales was moulded and planed
like boats on that two-tongued sea. Now an elegy

of cormorants lights across the tide,
and your people settle into bed with books
they do not speak, the dampened words
soaking into coast-sogged pages. Who calls the readers to climb

beyond the walls of poems, past Up Street and Down Street,
and sandstone purple as verbs? Who hues the boats
for their beautiful burning? *Son of the wave*
who never learned to swim, our voices lower

into pauses at your names. You spoke Welsh
only in emptied places. On seaside streets cobbled with quiet,
I, too, hear that fugue of blue, the sounds
like hand-dyed wools spread on a beach to dry.

Above, in the hills of Glen Lough, maker of poems
meant to be said, you cried first in the company of echoes:

We are the Dead, the Dead, the Dead, the Dead.

II. The Heartland

Material

In a story my mother loved to quote,
the girl collects *bits of people*—files of fingernails,
plastic baggies of hair. Is it any wonder

my two favorite words for years were *bizarre*
and *bazaar*, with their odd doubled letters,
the marked marketplace where my mother bartered

the freakish and true? A Navajo girl fled
boarding school with only a quart can of tuna;
a man drove head-on into an unlit train

and then returned, swaddled in plaster,
as though he disbelieved with every broken bone.

In Texas, a boy tipped headfirst
into a rain barrel, while in New York, a child smothered
inside a potted fern. My grandfather's ship exploded

in the South Pacific, killing every crewman plus their cook,
who, serving on a nearby ship, was struck with shrapnel.

Does this mean we'll all go at our time, or to move
cautiously in a world zigzagged with lightning?

My mother left morals unstated.

That same Navajo girl once fell on the metal spikes
of a wall, tearing her leg like a seam

from ankle to crotch. I learned early that *ravel*
means the same as *unravel*. Their opposite is *stitch*,
like the heavy threads of a wound.

When my mother took me to the fabric store,
I played among bolts of lace and gauze
while the saleswomen unspooled arm-lengths of cloth

and deftly cut—Lachesis and Atropos, estimating the shape
of human lives with raspy bric-a-brac shears.

Only one fate, Clothos, wove life into being.
From this, we get the word *fabricate*: to make cloth, to lie.

Heartlines

Listen to your heart, this new man tells me. We are in a bar
with red velvet curtains for walls, sashes of conversation

draped under music. He pours rum and then Coke over ice,
which rattles like elegant gravel. When I listen to my heart,

I hear tires crunching on a dirt road years out of this city:
thrum-pulse of wood slats on the high-water bridge. I swam

after angel fish in that shallow creek, and though I'm sure
now they were trout, or less, I remember their fins' flirtatious

silver. Why is it that blood, which is most of our bodies,
disappears when we strike it with light? If I could, I'd spend

this night in my own heart, hear its off-metronome gurgle,
flowing and falling of darkness. I'd string bright lure, open

and fill the locks. In there, my father's fibrillated beat,
my mother's paling blood. In the red-lit elevator, he jokes

clever-drunkenly of Dante, though next day, riding down
nine floors in silence, I do not think of hell,

but of a heart—awkwardly standing in a single chamber
as the cables lower us into our outside skins. I never see

this man again: a classical pianist stockbroker who promised
to seduce me with music. I remember these notes

like the seventy-five counties of a state I seldom visit, useless
even when I learned them as a child, unforgettably, by heart.

Two Drafts Written After a Fight

I.
Do I love you: *yes* or *no*?
The question: Is love a figure of speech?

I do—sometimes. Everyone wonders about our love; still,
there can be no doubt I have been true (almost always).

Happily remembering the start of our romance; it seemed
so promising . . .

And is love continual happiness or not?
Is *not* what matters?

I cannot tell you who I want to spend my life with.

Enough about our love.

II.
Do I love you? *Yes* or *no*—the question is, love,
a figure of speech. I do.

(Sometimes everyone wonders.)
About our love, still, there can be no doubt.

I have been true, almost always happily
remembering the start of our romance;

it seemed so promising, and is. Love,
continual happiness or not is not what matters.

I cannot tell you, who I want to spend my life with,
enough about our love.

Language Lessons

The carpet in the kindergarten room
was alphabet blocks; all of us fidgeting
on bright, primary letters. On the shelf
sat that week's inflatable sound. The *Th*
was shaped like a tooth. We sang
about brushing up and down, practiced
exhaling while touching our tongues
to our teeth. Next week, a puffy *U*
like an upside-down umbrella; the rest
of the alphabet deflated. Some days,
we saw parents through the windows
to the hallway sky. *Look, a fat lady*,
a boy beside me giggled. Until then
I'd only known my mother as beautiful.

Arkansas Churches

As the atheists' daughter, I had an open invitation to be lost
at ten different churches. Heaven was offered once each year

like pastel dresses for Easter, but Hell was ongoing. I followed
friends to leased one-story buildings: folding chairs and dark

paneling, Sunday School pitchers of Kool-Aid swirling like snow
globes, and in the unpaved parking lots' dusty heat, Satan

gunning to drive at our hearts. Methodists lined up Dixie cups
of grape juice, mouthwash for sinners; Southern Baptists prayed

fervently over mayonnaise salads. Even the Unitarians repented
when the ballet teacher who rented them her studio was found

by her husband, suddenly home on military leave, having sex
against the mirror with her lover. Reverend Bicks, of First

Baptist, made house calls in his suit the color of dried blood.
He drank mint tea in our kitchen evenings for weeks and shook

his Bible, in its gilded blue plastic cover, at my mother. It was
only a matter of time. Hell in all the homemade and store-bought

temptation of a potluck table; hell in the pines down snaking
gravel roads; hell beside the highway, concrete lawn ornaments

and cut-glass rocks, forest service towers where tourists paid
to imagine fire. My friends at Christ Church raced each other

through Bibles with butterfly pages, fingers skimming centuries
of stories I knew vaguely from felt boards, numbered apostles,

blackberry thickets of syllables, *Corinthians, Ecclesiastes,*
resting at last on the preordained chapter and verse. They too

had been bookmarked for salvation, remembered like light
switches in dark rooms, while I found myself in each dim,

carpeted lobby with a handful of welcome pamphlets and dollar
of my allowance to pay for knowing the ways I was damned.

Broken Engagements

Even though history never repeats itself, it does tend to rhyme.
—Mark Twain

I miss the boy with invisible crowbars who weekly asked,
Are you still married? Are you still happily married? No, yes. Yes, no.

Yes, we were good together, the way that words rhyme together
with no more shared meaning than if you say each one alone.

Only he would think to steal red velvet curtains by draping them
around a woman. The perfect affair: enter naked, wrap in velvet, go.

We were going to be married on a ship with red sails. I remember
the rigging, the polished rails, the deck that finally didn't hold.

We held each other's hearts like handmade vases; they broke
like Pfaltzgraff china. The pattern is still available, I'm told.

My ex-fiancé once told my future husband: *You use 'god'*
to such good effect in sentences. Don't I, god, now know.

So he will know: I left with certain words. I'm returning all
except the ones not here, plus *precious, cilantro, love,* a second *go.*

Bay Window, with Divorce and Pigeon

Just after the notary's kanji signature, his soft blue
stamp, my husband unbecoming my husband

(I wouldn't have believed it if I hadn't
been there), I walked into my living room

with the folder of papers and found the window broken
in a wide, symmetrical circle—glass sprayed

across the hardwood, under the couch, amid the tufts
of the white, wool shag we had bought together—

long slivers, jagged, improbable, and perfectly clear
as if the sky itself had exploded at the third story,

streaking white-green yolk of bird shit on the floor,
shattering ice from the August streetlamps, opening

a hole in the latched window, while in the fireplace,
eyeing me through cold black eyes, a single pigeon.

Unbloodily alive, its iridescent feathers matted.
I wanted to kill it for surviving, messenger of the obvious

flaws in the world's construction: in love's shelter,
we forgot the most luminous rooms have thin glass.

After the Crash

I drift from room to room,
switching on each fluorescent light,
the radiance thin and white as surgical gloves.
I water the jade from a stemmed glass.

A woman found two miles offshore this morning
believes she's a mermaid. She refused rescue,
saying, *I've just surfaced a minute for air.*

My body is an aquarium where gravel and fins
scrape in the darkness. When I breathe,
my ribs snare with coral. The glass pulled from my mouth
left no cuts.

I do not confess gratitude
for having newly shaved thighs
when they lifted me onto the gurney.

I'm adapting to ocean living
the woman said when they pulled her on deck,
fully dressed. *I'm adapting.*

I drift under my blue down comforter
for days without bathing.
Honey, I say, *we never know*
in time to be afraid.

Weeds

By the weed-science laboratory, someone has mown around dandelions—
each inflorescence bursting to yellow.

My soon-to-be-ex husband calls at midnight with lists of art books.
Do I remember? Do I want to remember?

I remember rusted trumpet vine and reflective paint, spilled
like a pearlescent prom dress on the road.

What seem to be grape vines have overtaken the oaks,
green skins of clouds soaking in Spanish barrels.

The year we've lived in Florida, I have never looked up a single plant.
The books I want to keep I never owned.

I drive through casks of daylight toward the Castillo de San Marcos,
its reenacted 16th-century masses banned after a tourist
    asked to take communion.

Weeds, says the used field-guide, have no essential definition:
any plant not valued where it is growing.

Nose Bleeds

When I was the poor girl at the private school, I imagined the rich
living at higher altitudes where the air was thinner. This explained
why the girls with new penny loafers lay like swooning princesses
in the nurse's office, their heads tilted back, nostrils trickling red
threads of refinement. They would return to class, collars stained,
Russian royalty like the hemophiliac Romanovs of whom I was
only a namesake, not an heir. At recess in winter, snow-white
kleenex drifting from pockets, white rabbit fur jackets. Years later,
my classmate, daughter of Texas's largest fur fortune, stabbed
her father to death for money and was sentenced for life. She'd played
the mother in our 4th-grade melodrama. As her daughter, the heroine,
I could pretend to be frail. My nose never bled, no matter how
I willed thick veins to weaken. I blamed my mother, granddaughter
of a housekeeper, our ruddy bloodline that kept surviving surviving.

Turning

Have I scared you with the God stuff?

my first ex writes. *I hope not. Because
He loves you.* He has sent a letter in tongues:

*Avea ono hastea anashea em shalie. Say this
deep in yourself, and your heart may be turned*

into a heart of flesh. On the night the car wrecked,
we'd eaten at the Krishna house by campus.

Three lanes away, through drizzle, headlights.
I started to say, *Do you see?* I started to say,

Wait, but I had left the words in an earlier
fight. *Avea ono hastea anashea em shalie.*

Now he wants to save me from drowning;
he has dreamed I am under lakewater,

struggling all these years after the night
I let us spin onto the sidewalk, glass raining,

mouth acrid with lentils, my body peeled
like Krishna's bathing maidens in Emergency.

Where were the eyes of any watchful god
when he had held me upside down

three floors above the lawn—
green tree frogs, pink stucco, blood searching

for a way from my head? I don't remember
what he was yelling, not one word I said

when he turned my flesh heart upright.

The Heartland

In the beginning was snow, fluffy and colored
like cabbage. Pale green leaves of light
folded in toward the ground.

We who were from nowhere
changed zip codes often, moving
into uncertain weather. The sameness of change

never ceased to astound us. Blocks away,
the American Ice Company's red bricks
melted to white. It was possible to believe

a whole city's snow came from inside.
Sidewalks turned into tightropes. The sky waited.
We all had something we'd rather stayed buried.

We all had something staked on the thaw.
One morning, the mailbox backed up
with forwards, which overflowed

down the steps. We'd been located by names
that chapped our lips when we said them.
Ice hung from the gutters of the art museum

like sculptures. People paid to stay outside.
Shovels made soft sweeps, brushes
across the unalterable, as men poured salt

to our doorstep, a great evaporated sea.
The papers tallied up deaths
and reported freezing was variable.

In Houston, people start dying
when the temperature drops below thirty,
while in Anchorage, death starts

at minus five. We had become
the midpoint of a mortal geography.

Kansas City

That winter, I waited tables
at a sports bar; I waited while
my mother died; she'd given up
cooking. She'd lost her appetite,
but still we'd meet at Houston's—
ostentatious jazz, plates clattering,
the mirrors above the leather
booths too high to see our faces:
tired and tired. The maître d'
who seated us looked balding
and small, but I'd seen him stun
in a black silk dress and heels.
That underground club had a rat
á la Chuck E. Cheese, raffling
something under strobes, twitching
those enormous whiskers. The city
was frozen then. I was vanilla-vodka
drunk as always. And the maître d'
was beautiful in ways we women
never hope for. Tall platters tottered
toward us like the Chinese acrobat
I once watched steady a teacup
on a slender stick: a plate; a cup; a plate;
a candle. What amazed me most
was how I no longer felt amazed
when piece by piece he disassembled
to that one small cup. We ordered
artichokes in oceans of butter,
pyres of french fries, anything
á la mode. It was the last season.
Iced brick streets; clamoring beats,
asking, *Do you believe in life after love?*

Measures

When my mother hated me, she left and drove.
Once, with a blizzard blowing in, she won
two tickets to the symphony; she'd stopped
a mile away and called the radio to name
a piece by Liszt. She recognized returning
as an art, practiced by leaving. She played

the piano rarely, said she'd never played
with grace, so taught instead. Her students drove
for miles, carrying folded music, returning
years later with stories of scholarships they'd won.
And those who can't do, teach. I learned the name
of every note, the sharps and flats; but stopped

just short of music, started over, stopped
again at thirteen, claiming Bon Jovi played
better than Van Cliburn. I'd learned to name
distance with music, although I only drove
my mother to smile, the fight already won
by age. I would grow up, she'd keep returning

from leaving, like a fugue's anger returning
to conscious quiet. One summer night she stopped
and bought two pints of ice cream; *vanilla won
against staying gone*, she said, as if she'd played
both hands. She never did say where she drove.
We knew the world inside was too vast to name,

so fled it. Before I could tell time, she'd name
an hour *two piano lessons*, turning
all distance into sound. My mother drove
a lesson more before we stopped;
my role was waiting while the time was played
in treble fields and roads until sleep won.

Stretched out across the backseat that I'd won
by default as the only child, I'd name
the constellations silently re-played
outside the glass each night, as if returning
were recital for a better leaving.
I learned its movements while my mother drove.

She and I never won the game that drove
us; never dared to name the song that really stopped
us; how our hearts played *allegro con spiritu* returning.

Threads

You'd think hands were enough to mend heartbreak
to see Frida holding hands with herself, scissors
in her left right hand. She has looped her artery

around both sides of her neck like a stethoscope
so she can listen to the rasp of lace
her chest makes as she cuts it open. Now her heart

sprouts like a brash corsage against the wedding
white, her skirt stained with blood,
stains forming petals, petals reforming

a hem of roses. In the garden outside
her frog-faced sons swing on imaginary
ropes, shoot arrows at glass medicine bottles;

to see their oversized hands, you would believe
hands could break the world, square
glass pane from pane out of its casement

the way their father's workers lift a whole sky
of blue agave and carry it singing
on the hills of their shoulders. Now the women

mop the tiles at the Ministry of Education,
a sundial of suds shifting across the courtyard.
Diego has wrapped the balcony above

their grey ropes with a single red ribbon,
like an inside-out present, one long poem
of progress bannering the great machines, the fists

clenching wrenches; Frida herself with her heart
back under a man's workshirt, carrying
a rifle and a stack of papers. She has left the yarn

of herself unraveled in her twin's lap,
and in this future, slim-hipped and childless
as the rifle itself, she uses the two hands he gives her.

II.
I take the pink silk ribbon she hands me,
unspool the length of my imagination, a little longer.
Pivoting, my friend models her pregnant belly

to the shower of women. Whoever can cut
to her precise circumference will win
a beautiful something: chocolate strawberries

on longstem skewers, a cookbook, a baby. *Your present
is at the end of this ribbon*, my mother told me
on my seventh birthday. Around the floor lamp,

handmade cloth of the dining-room table, tin hutch of cups, spice-
cake baking, kitchen to porch, swing, steps
past the chicken coop, the fountain's concrete shells

brimming with city water pumped like a secret
from its center to ribbon threaded dry
among iris and chainlink, one line mapping our double lot

like the AAA women made the future
we'd asked for visible, highlighting the highways
in clear, predestined pink. The baby doll

behind the garage looked up from her carriage
with closed lashes, her cheeks unripe and hard
as apples. Storebought, smelling sweetly

of plastic, she was a stranger in a family of yarn,
the first doll my mother hadn't sewn, the first
and last infant. When I held her for pictures, she blinked

blank and wistful for the box we both wished
she'd return to. I want to say this is how I first found
my limits, following the ribbon my mother spooled

maternally through dawn, the way I know now
even as the scissors shear: the pink silk I've measured
is longer than one body, but not enough for two.

III.
Longer than one body, but not enough for two,
the dress that peasant Frida wears
ends in Austrian lace. The bodice is blue

and gold for her Mexican mother;
her twin, she confides in her journal,
was conceived from her imaginary girlhood friend.

I told her my secret problems. Which ones?
I do not remember.
But from my voice she knew everything about me.

Now they clasp hands below a sky of milk
churned with thunder, their hair braided
in high, tight crowns in case women start raining again,

white swan-diving bodies; plastic bathing caps
cinched around firm chins. My imaginary friend
rode a motorcycle through our kitchen,

cursing like a sailor while my mother baked.
She was everything beyond me,
words I didn't know, tearing up and down

the linoleum of the hospital hallway
where the nuns left my mother, sixteen when my first
sister was born, threading her with blood

to a loveless marriage. Sometimes, now
my mother leans across the table of dreams
to take my hand between both of her palms,

like I am a picture in a locket. We both know
she is dead, but it doesn't matter,
bowls of minestrone and spoons before us,

the morphine re-capped in its bottle. From my voice,
she knows everything about me. From her touch,
I'd think hands were enough to mend heartbreak.

III. PRESENT PERFECT

Levels

We're looking for that sure thing: the glowing yellow
of a carpenter's level with its bead of oil,
or is it air, that promises perfection, and we know

tonight we'll never hold it steady, like the ladder
in an old song I loved when I was far too young
to understand *James, James, hold the ladder*

steady, and my mother had to explain *eloping*
because I didn't yet know the edges of my life
so well I'd want to climb outside it—hanging

on only a promise; I still get lost on familiar
blocks, the sun not gone, but leaving, floating
crookedly down between the buildings, or

maybe we've built the ground slantingly
from landfills as all conversations tend to become
lopsided, even the most romantic or especially

the most romantic; she was ready, which rhymed
of course, but I can't remember how it ended,
if he really held her steady on the long climb

to the bottom rung, and why she had to call
his name twice as if he might not really be
there—the ladder just sprouted like a tall

tree against her window, and her stepping off
backwards and singing into the rest of her life.

Choose-Your-Own-Adventure Poem

To find a bird metaphor go to stanza twenty;
to find an ocean metaphor go to stanza six.

To follow the heroine through the jungle ruins
of Tikal, her camera loaded with the wrong speed of film,

howler monkeys bellowing at the thunder, and the rain coming
through the canopy like a vast lace umbrella, turn to the second couplet,

although you may also arrive on that slippery clay trail, roots
    breaking apart the stairs
of civilization itself, if you start with a line

about a modern city: traffic stalling amid angled glass buildings,
stop signs graffitied with personal instructions: *Stop Driving, Stop Stopping,*
Stop Us. If you are seeking only the lines that launched the heroine

into this poem, as though on a small boat—used weekdays
    for commercial fishing
but hosed of blood on Sundays for sighting whales and sea birds
with lungs in their wings—

then stop at the first couplet, although now that you have chosen
to go further, you can learn that their original author (who worries that
his real last name, *Champagne*, sounds like a pseudonym and will
therefore be referred to as *Smith*)

appears again in what will later be revealed as a love story.

If, on the other hand, you are concerned more with form than content,
with raking the gravel of your soul
into a Japanese garden;

if you would like to ponder rocks shaped like cranes shaped like
    continents shaped like turtles
and watch the heroine walk hand in hand with another man
    under clear plastic umbrellas,

the rain seeming to fall in their dry hair,

suspecting that despite this temporary suspension, the sky *is* falling,
the boards of the temples rotting into leaves of green tea,

the love story that they had chosen forever ending
as they sit in perfectly formed silence below the temple scaffolding,
as they scald themselves feverish red in the public bathhouse,
as though to bring their hearts back
into their bodies,

then you can work backwards to the jungle where the rain becomes
a cold sweat.

If you choose this route, you will not watch her pack souvenir scarves
around her half of their dishes, silk made to look like rocks made
    to look like waves,
one morning in the angular light of the city.

Or, for a more metaphoric and therefore beautiful ending,
you may continue past the awful still waves of those scarves
on a boat that has just hit deep water
above the continental shelf when a whale surfaces
   with its black lace flukes

and the camera falls overboard,

and the heroine doesn't care because she is holding the hand of a man
named *Smith*, newly introduced with his soaking shoes
and black peacoat, the boat pitching more slowly

than her blood, which she realizes is suddenly returning all at once
from their hands to her heart,

as though she is, after all, the kind of resilient
   seabird the naturalist has shown them:
one with lungs in its wings.

From *The Spell Tables*

The game features humankind for a reason.
It is the most logical basis in an illogical game.
—Advanced D&D Dungeon Master's Guide

We don't talk about all that we believe
we can do, the seams of magic underneath:

the odds for Augury and Sleep, Slow Poison
or Resisting Fire. We have seen others Pass without a Trace,

Feign Death, Regenerate. We know the words
we would not say in public: the ones we Speak with Plants

or use to Transmute Rock to Mud. Inside our heads are landslides;
all of us have been there buried. Our resumés may prophecy our skills

in other terms, but who doesn't mean to say, *I Call Lightning
and Charm Person or Mammal. . . Here is my number.*

If pressed, we'd all admit we Speak with Monsters. We know Holy
and Unholy Word so equally we sometimes can't tell which is which;

we feel Creeping Doom more often than Continual Light,
and seek, everywhere, Symbol. Others, we suspect, have studied longer

or better, mastering the spells of single words. Do we have to start there,
or can we use Word of Recall to Reincarnate, Time Stop,

Speak with Dead? These are not party tricks or sleights of hand
but where we'd start if we were playing by our rules. We who were raised

on stories of Part Water, Insect Plague, and Cure Disease
have come too late. The showy spells have all been done before.

We have watched Snake Charm, practiced Pyrotechnics.
We only need the manual now for common spells:

Comprehend Languages, Change Self, Hold Person.

Four Games Played While Riding the Bus

I.
The couple across the aisle is playing Rock, Paper, Scissors.
Over and over their hands touch. Under and over,
and Rock is always beaten by Paper's soft drapery,
though Rock's crushing of Scissors has more military
pomp, while Scissors are always a cut above Paper.
The elegance of childhood rules defining nature.
Amazing, I think, not that adults would play,
but that the game has brought into the rush-hour fray
this tacit silence: each one deciding only as they move
the shapes their own fists guard. With each smooth
sleight of hand, they're turning *It's better like this;
it's not. Let's don't. Let's do. My love, I know your tricks;
You never will* . . . into swift One, Two, Three.
Each turn risking strength exposed as vulnerability.

II.
Maybe Alzheimer's is angelic possession,
the mind's repetitive wings beating sense
for all it's worth. *God-damn talking bus.*
God-damn talking bus, says the old man
at each announcement. And doesn't everyone
agree really, though our askance glances impress
that calls for silence ought to come in silence?
Please vacate front seats for seniors—God-damn
talking bus—*and the disabled.* Each sing-song
echo more mechanical, we raise embarrassed
newspapers or drink from empty coffee cups.
But after he climbs off and the voice goes on,
No eating or drinking on Muni, someone says
below their breath, *Oh, won't you just shut up?*

III.
The French-Algerian self-proclaimed genius painter
in a scarf and burgundy fedora on the hottest October
evening this San Francisco reasons, *But I'm not wearing
any socks or underwear*, and he shows us by baring
his ankles, adding, *six pieces, counting my shoes*.
After the quiet minute in which we each, impromptu,
tally, one friend says *seven*, another *five*, and I, blushing,
four, and just like that—fully dressed—lose. The evening
is down to hairpins of light outside the bus windows,
the plastic seats smooth as skin, and in the seconds that follow
this shared revelation, we ride silently toward the dark
as though we have found a new, more serious art:
not to paint the town, but to watch it, hour by hour, strip,
each loss wagered on this companionship.

IV.
Near the back of the bus, a man sits down and deals
three cards into his lap. One, the king, is marked.
He says, *These two lose, the king card wins. These
two lose, the king card wins. Not these; the red card.
If you got money and you got heart, you can win
yourself some money now*. With shuffling sleight
of hand, he turns them up, but no one will play him.
The king is bent. *These two lose, the king card's high.
If you got twenty, and you got heart*. Will no one play
because the game is rigged to favor us, because we
pity him his fumbling fast hands as they lay
the bent card down, or do we fear the con that surely
waits? No matter the cards, we know these blues:
if you got money and you got heart, you can always lose.

Hurricane Season

When I become accustomed at last to lying in bed alone,
    sheets finely wrinkled as curtains blown across the windows

of dreams, and the crane-necked streetlight fills the room
    with its electric-nerved, luminous vision, what I had

seen for my future (the restless flowering of his arms in sleep
    around my shoulder, the soiled pillows in their matching cases

where our faces, breaths apart, turned toward and away) recedes
    like the hurricane that never hit land the night we met,

when the beach was evacuated, the buildings shuttered in plywood,
    and the news crews stood dry amid the whipping palms,

in the margins of their own story. Later, we saw a photograph shot
    high in the clouds: the storm's eye turning above the ocean,

as we swam at midnight in the pool naked, waiting to be swept up
    in a chlorine shudder, a geyser of winds, into the rapture

of our lives. And though we almost bought it together, we didn't.
    Somewhere, framed in its calm bay of glass, that storm is hanging—

on the gallery's wall at the pinpoint end of this land, or in a room
    like the one where even now he is lying beside her, sleep's

aperture narrowing around them, and all the years when we almost
    loved each other forever, at last, blown far off the shore of this life.

By Special Arrangement

The pink mylar fish balloon, floating stringless above the streets,
three buckets of irises, the last to be taken in at the flower shop

as though waiting for me, my favorites, the wind gusting the long
harp strings of the telephone wires as the man in a nice jacket

leads the homeless woman home, their story my invention
but still I believe she is his mother and he has found her here

on the red-brick skid row of Market, his hand patting the blanket
on her back, his whispers reassuring her that she is who he calls her,

another woman yelling up to a friend as she goes down the escalator
to the subway, lingeringly disappearing like a comic exit,

floating gracefully down a river of stairs, one person on the surface
worth recalling as she drowns, the trolleys passing on hammered

straight rails, and none of this having any direct bearing on my day
shifting toward evening on the round faces of the up-set clocks,

their poles rooted in brick. If only the ground were water
as the Alhambra's architects believed half of each place should be,

the reflections would be real as stone, and we'd see the numbers
swimming up below us, the ticking of minutes rippling

at our shoes, and we'd remember this has all been arranged,
though maybe not for us, and maybe by special accident—

a singing telegram of love misdelivered to this city, hardened
as it is against incursions of beauty, though not immune,

as the strip-club marquees announce *Your Wildest Fantasies
Are Inside Now*, and the men who never seem to enter

exit on the street before me, their stride as purposeful and fast
as apostles sent to preach the truth into the wilds of this evening.

Woman on Train at Night in the Desert

You must learn to see so much beauty, unarranged,
with only your eyes.
          —Georgia O'Keeffe

Precipitate violet, the dark came rushing headlong
down the tracks. The sky borrowed nothing from memory.

In the watermarked night she'd sent him rolled in a tube,
the flecked paper stars had shone through aquarelle

like her studio's one bare bulb. After months of charcoal,
she was certain only of space and erasures. The smoke bloomed

now into its own horizon. *At last, a woman on paper,* he'd written;
this woman, who knelt to draw lines and smudges

while the Palo Duro seethed outside like warm cut fruit.
The platform lights wavered and straightened

across indigo seats. She'd forgiven those intimate hollows
he'd hung against burlap, but was she not herself so many lines,

a distraction from war? In his dreams, he wrote her, *Woman*
had wild, nearly blank eyes and wrote death boldly on walls.

She ate as though starved for colors.

English Fundamentals

To practice her grammar, Hee-Sun is diagramming
the Bible's most beautiful sentences. She brings me
Consider the lilies of the field in small, neat script.
She does not say if she believes the gospels, just

The language is so pretty, shyly asking if the subject
is implied. Are *lilies* and *field*—drawn inside green
rectangles—different kinds of objects? Each day
for months, I've watched her arrange the morning

colors from her narrow case of pens: laying them
like scalpels for the body of her new language.
She loves inverted subjects and elliptical clauses:
rare cases that reveal new, more subtle workings.

But now, as I see each word made radiant, *Consider
grow, toil,* and *spin* underlined in purple, *And yet
I say to you* circled in red, I see the colors are tools
of a more ancient reverence. She has handed me

grammar as a stained glass window, each piece cut
and soldered into syntax. *Even Solomon* (proper
noun, blue as a subject) *in all his glory* (hot pink
prepositional phrase) *was not arrayed like one of these.*

Gandhi on the Oakland Ferry

Before this particular bridge slung its low horizon
waterward from sky, and the shipping docks creaked
with the metal weight of crates being hoisted from ships,
human-size toy cars unloading from sardine-can boxes;

before the cranes with their white necks and pulleys
lifted our eyes from the wake, and fog banked in closer,
the spires of skyscrapers floating toward us on a raft
of electric grey, an island of glass and erasures; before

turning away from the city we had left; before climbing
the stairs from the last, low holds of jazz; before the wind
with its pith of salt and desire, our numb hands on the rail,
and the cocktail glasses clinking below us, we had stood

at the base of the city, at the paved edge of land, and seen
a man with his bronze walking stick raised, a diviner's rod
for all oceans, for the tides of we who would come, molten
and frozen and human. We had watched him stepping down

from his pedestal, over the inscriptions of waves, composed
amid the throng of bicycles and men on the rattling gangplank,
standing sandal-footed on the empty deck beside us in his thin
clothing of fog, as we crossed to the dusk and lights of Oakland.

Today, Act II

Scene I

A young, Black student tells the class he's seen
Desdemona being chased by Iago through the Mission's streets:
her in broken plastic sandals; him in a t-shirt with stains,

shouting above the hawking of churros: *Woman,*
Let thy soul be instructed, as she puts her tongue in her heart
and slips behind a hanging carpet patterned with a pride
of lions.
           And though I need to return us to Cyprus:
the tall warships of Turkey newly sunk; the sudden storm
dissipated into long foreshadows; and Iago pursuing his game
through snares of language; everything that is seeming otherwise,

I imagine Desdemona peeking out to see the coast
has cleared, and threading her way amid the discount bins
of linens, picking a handkerchief and throw pillow.

Scene II

A headline in the Bay Area section: *Mom, 23, charged
with murdering 2 babies.* I do not want to be morbidly intrigued
yet find myself reading *she smothered them because they cried;*
she was *tired of noise.* She was seeking, with her pillow,
some silence.

                Two years ago, she carried a baby
unconscious to the hospital, and now the scene repeats:
clean sheets after months on the street,
a baby wailing. *The very seamark of her utmost sail.* Then,

quiet, as when the men at the lighthouse cannons
went abruptly deaf in the midst of their own warnings
(fog has shrouded the rocks and shipwreck is likely).
Neither autopsy found evidence of struggle,
her confession, the only way *we know for sure there was foul play.*

Present Perfect

My students understand better
if I draw a timeline—horizon

with two ends, shorthand
for anything short of infinity.

I mark the brief rules of past,
present, future; arc a line

linking the past and now: the tense
with a name so lovely

and misleading we'd all like
to describe (stepping out

onto my third-floor landing;
pigeons swooping over chimneys

like pigeons in every time; the hills
massed into lilac clouds; the vertigo

of sky opening at eye level;
scattered lights of lives

carrying on their private
anchorage) something entirely

and not-that-much different
from perfection. As *I have lived*

all my life in this world, and still
it surprises me. Why not

I lived in this world? Gratified
each time someone answers,

In the second, you lived
in the past, but you're standing

up there in the present, too, alive.

Color Theory

The Home Depot salesman says, "Remember, you won't
have to live *with* your choice: You'll have to live
        inside it." I imagine each gradation—unpacking

frying pans and toothbrush; paperbacks strewn
inside Plum Wine, Arctic Lilac, Chiasmic Violet.
        On the glossy card they've chained beside the racks

of color, I learn that purple promotes drowsiness and nausea:
not recommended for kitchens or the pilothouse
        of boats. Yellow, while energizing, can make one irritable,

unable to blink naturally, too anxious to swallow. Which shade
is it that makes one likely to remember turns
        from years-ago samba classes, make perfect hollandaise,

sing like Bernadette Peters? Which color will help me find
my mother's citrine ring (borrowed and lost
        in seventh grade) or remember the name of the Australian

band that sang "A Girl," or find the hotel where Klimt awoke
in a light sweat after dreaming *The Kiss*?
        If I paint the living room First Green and the office

Eggshell and Mist, what primordial creatures will hatch
from the doorway clouds, what storm fronts
        sweep my bookcases empty? Will my insurance refuse

payment for accidents resulting from color—the Supernova Blue
that caused me to fly kites from second-floor
        windows or the Miami Sunburst trimmed with Japonica

that enticed me to juggle butcher knives and pomegranates?
To make things simple, I'd like one color
         that will make me want to sing, cry, fuck, write letters

to strangers, wear fishnet stockings, buy irises, walk barefoot,
listen to Coltrane, move out, stay forever,
         have children, and understand winter. One can, well stirred.

Love Poem

for Dylan

Today, I passed our favorite house
on the walk to groceries: slate-colored wood;

the witch-hat roof your ex said was ghastly,
is not, as you always knew.

Three stories: windows plus windows
plus the tower, solid,

and when it narrows into sky—exclamatory.
The tree seems to be flying, branches on both sides

of the lawn like a tree in a windstorm in a painting,
and everything is in bloom beneath it,

even the gravel. If this is hyperbole, it is
in the same way as grand pianos

or mountains ranging the length of continents.
At night, the back sunroom glows

like a transparent quilt, small squares of glass
assembled when the world still felt worth celebrating

at World's Fairs: white crystal and electric bouquets.
A flight of dark pink stairs,

bolder than I would have chosen,
but right for its lot. True, it's strange,

but she was wrong about impractical.
I could imagine living here close-to-enough

before dying. Gothic, yes,
but in that comforting way, like Victrolas

in rosewood, or old photographs
of lovers kissing. I don't even know

the address or the owners, but it doesn't matter.
I have taken to calling it ours.

Performative Language

Because twice I corrected my fifth-grade teacher
with my natural science confidence of chipmunks,
chiming back, hand still raised like I held the helium of this fact
on a string I could not let go of, *but the book says*
so you're wrong, and he snapped *when you're the teacher,*
you can teach the classes, I am in the trough
before a wave of grown-up faces, chalk-stained skirt and heels
to make me feel taller, answering why the answer key
I instructed them to use is wrong. *Father is not,*
and never will be, an adverb. Remember persons, places, things. Actions.
Existences. Ways of doing. A toad-faced teacher in the Ozarks
who cursed his straight-A student straight
into this moment. Think of the fairytale logic
that allows this: the mother in The Seven Ravens banishing
her rowdy sons—*Oh that you would turn*
into seven black ravens and fly away from here—on the wings
of one imprecation, forgiving them back
into human bodies. *I forgive you. I do.*
I apologize. This is not a fairytale. This is more
than karma, the kingdom of language
with its slippery keys. Each small stone constructs
ripples. *You cannot do an action*
in a father way, meaning you can think hard or think slowly
but never think father. It is a noun. A verb.
My father fathered only one child. A girl. A raven.
Pray for me, Father. Think of this
as a chance to test your conviction
about the nature of the simplest words.

Précis

I am halfway around the lake before I can remember
the word *clam*; all the seagulls today with discs

in their beaks. Almost Christmas: strings of white
lights: pigeon, light, pigeon, light, pigeon.

The Hill Castle Apartment Hotel. So many names
strung together. The woman beside me on the train

was working on *The Inferno Examination*. Shopping
bags, stained fabric seats, boy with a hardcover

cookbook. In the tunnel, our faces flashing. Houses.
Question 1: Supply the Allegorical Meaning.

A Christmas tree floating on a raft. A yard with a plastic
crèche. Dark at 4 p.m. in Oakland, winter, cornering

Grand. The lake's brilliant grey. Dirty feathers and lights.

King's Road, Bimini

At dusk on these islands, logic rough-velvet and green
as artichoke leaves pulls loose. A woman walks out across water,
stands barefoot on the burnish of tide. We both watch her feet,

though it's her arms she's moving, like she's calling back
light into its coop of mangroves, a big-boned fable

in an ordinary dress. When we look away, she keeps walking,
down the hot dishwasher-silver of our restaurant knives,
around the pooled feet of wine glasses, a one-woman road
to a revival on this shore that smells of fried shrimp and sea

and warm shampoo, a balcony cantilevered just over the end
of all sensible earth. It's already getting late to think of prayers,

like searching for salt on warm meat, while the shaker sits spillably
between us, and red cocktail sauce soaks the napkin's ruff
into a rooster's comb. Voodoo origami, plumed trash; sails clatter

and crow on the bight, and the lights of the few boats have been shunted
suddenly to heaven, leaving this common dark.

Acknowledgments

Thank you to the editors of the following journals in which these poems first appeared for believing in this work:

The Carolina Quarterly, "No Dominion"; *Crazyhorse*, "House Guest," "Levels," "Seeing Edward Hopper's *Hotel Room*"; *Epoch*, "Woman on Train at Night in the Desert"; *The Iowa Review*, "Present Perfect," "Two Drafts Written After a Fight"; *The Mangrove Review*, "After the Crash"; *Mid-American Review*, "The Eucharist," "Choose-Your-Own-Adventure Poem"; *The Missouri Review*, "Bay Window, with Divorce and Pigeon," "Frames," "Kansas City," "The Heartland," "Four Games Played While Riding the Bus"; *New England Review*, "Cork," "Heartlines," "Threads"; *New Letters*, "Broken Engagements," "By Special Arrangement," "Hiking Through: The John Muir Trail"; *Notre Dame Review*, "Dead Reckoning," "Performative Language," "English Fundamentals"; *The Paris Review*, "Cave Tours"; *Puerto del Sol*, "Notes from the Twelfth Week: May 1676"; *Quarterly West*, "King's Road, Bimini"; *Slate*, "Adjectives of Order"; *Southern Poetry Review*, "Material" (as "Patterns"); *Third Coast*, "Language Lessons"; *32 Poems*, "What I Know for Sure," "Nose Bleeds"; *The Threepenny Review*, "The Idea of North"; *Valparaiso*, "Hurricane Season."

Thank you to the editors of the following anthologies and publications in which these poems were reprinted:

American Life in Poetry, "Language Lessons"; *Best American Poetry 2009*, "Heartlines"; *Best New Poets 2008*, "Adjectives of Order"; *Poetry Daily Essentials 2007*, "House Guest."

I am also very grateful to the many people without whose encouragement, insight, and wonderful suggestions for revision this book would not exist. Particularly, my deep thanks to my fellow poets at The University of Florida and the Stegner workshop, and to my professors—including William Logan, Eavan Boland, Ken Fields, and Simone Di Piero. Many thanks also to Michael Burns for first believing in my work; John Walsh for years of close reading; Alisa Messer and Elizabeth Bradfield for good advice; Gabriel Fried for insightful editing; and to my family, as well as all my colleagues, friends, and students at City College of San Francisco for sharing their stories and encouragement. Finally, unending thanks to my parents, Raymond and Sylvia Teague, and my stepmother, Bonnie Remsberg, for unconditional support and wise perspective. Love and thanks to Dylan Champagne for patiently and insightfully reading and re-reading, and for being a fantastic partner.

"For in what does time differ from eternity except we measure it," quoted in "Hiking Through," is from Anne Carson's poem "The Glove of Time by Edward Hopper."